WHOEVER
YOU ARE

WHOEVER YOU ARE

By MEM FOX   Illustrated by LESLIE STAUB

Voyager Books
Harcourt, Inc.
Orlando   Austin   New York   San Diego   Toronto   London

For information about permission to reproduce selections from this book, write to trade.
permissions@hmhco.com or to Permissions, Houghton Mifflin Harcourt Publishing
Company, 3 Park Avenue, 19th Floor, New York, New York 10016.

www.hmhco.com

First Voyager Books edition 2001

Voyager Books is a trademark of Harcourt, Inc., registered in the United States of America and/or other jurisdictions.

The Library of Congress has cataloged the hardcover edition as follows:
Fox, Mem, 1946–
Whoever you are/Mem Fox; illustrated by Leslie Staub.
p. cm.
Summary: Despite the differences between people around the world,
there are similarities that join us together, such as pain, joy, and love.
1. Ethnicity—Juvenile literature.   2. Multiculturalism—Juvenile literature.   3. Individual differences—Juvenile literature.
[1. Ethnicity.   2. Multiculturalism.   3. Individuality.]   I. Staub, Leslie, 1957– ill.   II. Title.
GN495.6.F69   1997
305.8—dc20   95-17887
ISBN-13: 978-0-15-200787-4   ISBN-10: 0-15-200787-3
ISBN-13: 978-0-15-206030-5 pb   ISBN-10: 0-15-206030-8 pb

SCP   25 24 23 22 21 20 19 18 17
4500643988

The illustrations in this book were done in oil on gessoed paper.
The hand-carved frames were made from plaster, wood, and faux gems.
The display type was hand-lettered by Judythe Sieck.
The text type was set in Monotype Goudy Bold
Color separations by Bright Arts Graphics Pte, Ltd., Singapore
Printed and bound by RR Donnelley
Production supervision by RR Donnelley
Designed by Judythe Sieck

For Hanan Ashrawi
—M. F.

For YaYa
and for you,
whoever you are
—L. S.

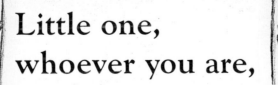

Little one,
whoever you are,

wherever you are,

there are little ones
just like you
all over the world.

Their skin may be different from yours, and their homes may be different from yours.

Their schools may be
different from yours,

and their lands may be
different from yours.

Their lives may be
different from yours,

and their words may be *very different from yours.*

But inside,
their hearts are
just like yours,

whoever they are,
wherever they are,
all over the world.

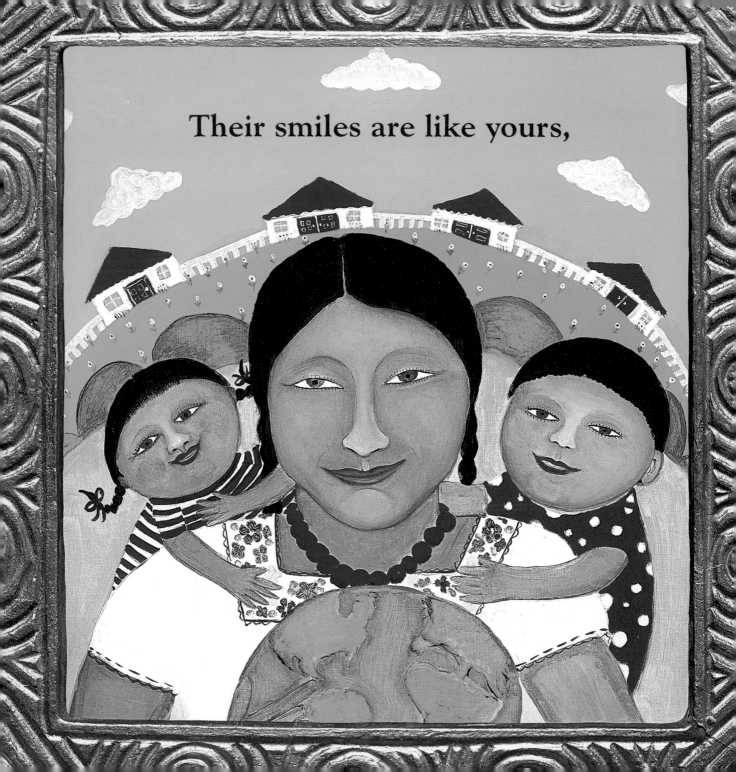

Their smiles are like yours,

and they laugh just like you.

Their hurts are like yours,
and they cry like you, too,

whoever they are,
wherever they are,
all over the world.

Little one,
when you are older
and when you are grown,

you may be different,

and they may be different,
wherever you are,
wherever they are,
in this big, wide world.

But remember this:

Joys are the same,
and love is the same.

Pain is the same,
and blood is the same.

Smiles are the same,
and hearts are just the same—
wherever they are,
wherever you are,
wherever we are,

all over the world.